big NATE

OUT LOUD

D1115982

big NATE OUT LOUD

by LINCOLN PEIRCE

SCHOLASTIC INC.
New York Toronto London Auckland
Sydney Mexico City New Delhi Hong Kong

No part of this publication may be reproduced, stored in a retrieval system, or transmitted in any form or by any means, electronic, mechanical, photocopying, recording, or otherwise, without written permission of the publisher. For information regarding permission, write to Andrews McMeel Publishing, LLC, an Andrews McMeel Universal company, 1130 Walnut Street, Kansas City, MO 64106.

ISBN 978-0-545-42702-9

Big Nate Out Loud copyright © 2011 by Lincoln Peirce. All rights reserved.
Published by Scholastic Inc., 557 Broadway, New York, NY 10012, by arrangement with Andrews McMeel Publishing, LLC, an Andrews McMeel Universal company. SCHOLASTIC and associated logos are trademarks and/or registered trademarks of Scholastic Inc.

12 11 10 9 8 7 6 5 4 3 2 11 12 13 14 15 16/0

Printed in the U.S.A. 23

First Scholastic printing, November 2011

These strips appeared in newspapers from April 2, 2007, through November 4, 2007.

For the Rhode Islanders

© 2007 by NEA, Inc.

© 2007 by NEA, Inc.

© 2007 by NEA, Inc.

© 2007 by NEA, Inc.

© 2007 by NEA, Inc.

© 2007 by NEA, Inc.

I LOVE THIS TIME OF YEAR! IT'S JOB-FREE!

JOB-FREE?
NO RESPONSIBILITIES, TEDDY!

THE SNOW HAS MELTED, SO THERE'S NOTHING TO SHOVEL...

THE GRASS HASN'T STARTED GROWING YET, SO THERE'S NOTHING TO MOW...

EFF ST
...AND THERE AREN'T ANY LEAVES ON THE GROUND, SO THERE'S NOTHING TO RAKE!

NO RESPONSIBILITIES! JOB-FREE!
WRIGHT

WHAT A REVOLTING TURN OF EVENTS.
DANG IT!

© 2007 by NEA, Inc.

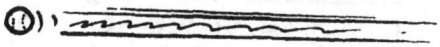

© 2007 by NEA, Inc.

© 2007 by NEA, Inc.

© 2007 by NEA, Inc.

© 2007 by NEA, Inc.

© 2007 by NEA, Inc.

WHAT'S UP, PEST?
THERE'S NOBODY TO PLAY CATCH WITH.

FRANCIS HAS A SWIM MEET... TEDDY IS VISITING HIS GRAND-PARENTS... NOBODY ELSE IS AROUND!

WHAT ABOUT DAD?
DAD?

SURE, ISN'T HE ALWAYS BUGGING YOU TO PLAY CATCH?

HE'D PROBABLY LOVE IT IF YOU ASKED HIM FOR A CHANGE!
HMM...

YOU'RE RIGHT, ELLEN! I'LL GIVE HIM ONE OF THOSE FATHER-SON MOMENTS AND TOTALLY MAKE HIS DAY!

DAD! HEY, DAD! WANNA HUCK A BALL AROUND?

I'M TRYING TO DO MY TAXES!

WANNA PLAY CATCH?
Peirce

© 2007 by NEA, Inc.

© 2007 by NEA, Inc.

© 2007 by NEA, Inc.

© 2007 by NEA, Inc.

© 2007 by NEA, Inc.

© 2007 by NEA, Inc.

CHESTER: PITCHING...
FRANCIS: CATCHING...
TEDDY: CENTER FIELD...
NATE: RIGHT FIELD...
AGAIN?
WELL, WHY NOT? YOU'RE A VERY GOOD RIGHT FIELDER!
YEAH, BUT...
NOTHING EVER HAPPENS OUT THERE!
THAT'S JUST THE WAY BASEBALL IS, NATE. SOMETIMES THEY HIT IT TO YOU, AND SOMETIMES THEY DON'T!
YEAH, I KNOW...
...BUT IT'S JUST SO BORING STANDING AROUND FOR NINE INNINGS!
JUST GET OUT THERE, NATE. I'M SURE YOU'LL FIND SOME WAY TO KEEP YOURSELF AMUSED.
COACH
Peirce

MRS. GODFREY SAYS THAT IF I DON'T START KEEPING MY DESK AND LOCKER CLEAN, IT'LL AFFECT MY GRADE!
BETTER NEATEN UP, DUDE.
I CAN'T! I'VE TRIED, BUT I CAN'T!
I'M JUST A MESSY PERSON! I WAS BORN MESSY!
WELL, TECHNICALLY, I THINK EVERYONE'S BORN MESSY.
YEAH, REMEMBER THAT MOVIE WE SAW IN HEALTH CLASS?
CAN WE TALK ABOUT SOMETHING ELSE?
© 2007 by NEA, Inc.

© 2007 by NEA, Inc.

© 2007 by NEA, Inc.

© 2007 by NEA, Inc.

© 2007 by NEA, Inc.

© 2007 by NEA, Inc.

NATE! WHAT DO YOU THINK YOU'RE DOING?
YOU TOLD ME TO KEEP MYSELF AMUSED.
NOT BY BRINGING A TROMBONE ONTO THE FIELD!
HOW DO YOU EXPECT TO PLAY BASEBALL WHEN YOU'RE...
KRAK!
CLANG!
HOME! HOME! HE'S COMIN' HOME!
BLAST!
WUMP!
Yer OUT!
!
WHAT WERE YOU SAYING?
Peirce

© 2007 by NEA, Inc.

© 2007 by NEA, Inc.

© 2007 by NEA, Inc.

© 2007 by NEA, Inc.

© 2007 by NEA, Inc.

© 2007 by NEA, Inc.

YANK!
SPUT! SPUT!
DANG IT!
ALLOW ME, DAD! ALLOW ME!
THEY CALL ME THE "MOWER WHISPERER"!
YANK!
RRRRR
WOW! WHAT DID YOU SAY?
SORRY, DAD! TRADE SECRET!
RRRRRR
NOW IF YOU'LL EXCUSE ME, MY JOB HERE IS DONE!
NOT QUITE.
!
RRRRRRRR

© 2007 by NEA, Inc.

© 2007 by NEA, Inc.

© 2007 by NEA, Inc.

© 2007 by NEA, Inc.

© 2007 by NEA, Inc.

© 2007 by NEA, Inc.

WELL! HELLO, NATE!
HI, MR. EUSTIS! WOULD SPITSY LIKE TO GO FOR A WALK?
I'M SURE HE'D LOVE IT!
GREAT! C'MON, SPITSY!
wurf!
HERE, LET ME GIVE YOU A COUPLE OF BUCKS.
NOPE! NOT TODAY!
I'M WORKING ON MY "GOOD NEIGHBOR" MERIT BADGE! I'M SUPPOSED TO DO RANDOM ACTS OF KINDNESS!
THIS ISN'T A PAYING JOB! THIS IS JUST TO BE NICE!
YANK!
FORGET THE BADGE. I'LL TAKE THE MONEY.
Peirce

© 2007 by NEA, Inc.

© 2007 by NEA, Inc.

© 2007 by NEA, Inc.

© 2007 by NEA, Inc.

© 2007 by NEA, Inc.

© 2007 by NEA, Inc.

FAKE FIGHT?
FAKE FIGHT!
POW!
OOF!

HYA!
ARRGH!
BOOF!
CHUCKLE!

FOOM!
HEY!

YOU CLIPPED ME FOR REAL!
OW!
SHOVE!

DON'T PUNK ME, MAN!
YOU STARTED IT, SCRUB!

LOOKS LIKE FUN, DOESN'T IT?
IF YOU SAY SO.
OW! I'M BLEEDING, YOU JERK!
JERK THIS, WUSSY BOY!
Peirce

© 2007 by NEA, Inc.

© 2007 by NEA, Inc.

© 2007 by NEA, Inc.

© 2007 by NEA, Inc.

© 2007 by NEA, Inc.

© 2007 by NEA, Inc.

I'VE BEEN TRYING ALL WEEK TO GET MR. GALVIN TO LAUGH, BUT IT'S IMPOSSIBLE!

I'VE TOLD HIM EVERY JOKE I KNOW! EVERY RIDDLE!!

...BUT NOTHING!
I CAN GET HIM TO LAUGH!

YOU?? SNORT! RIGHT, GINA!
I'LL BET YOU FIVE BUCKS!

YOU'RE ON!
FOLLOW ME!

MR. GALVIN, NATE THINKS HE HAS A GOOD CHANCE TO MAKE THE HONOR ROLL THIS TERM. WHAT DO YOU THINK?

WELL, I... MMMPH!
AHEM! CHUCKLE!... HEH HEH...

WA HA HA HA HA HA HA HA HA HA HA HA

OH, THE INDIGNITY.
YOU KNOW, THAT WAS WORTH FIVE BUCKS!
Peirce

© 2007 by NEA, Inc.

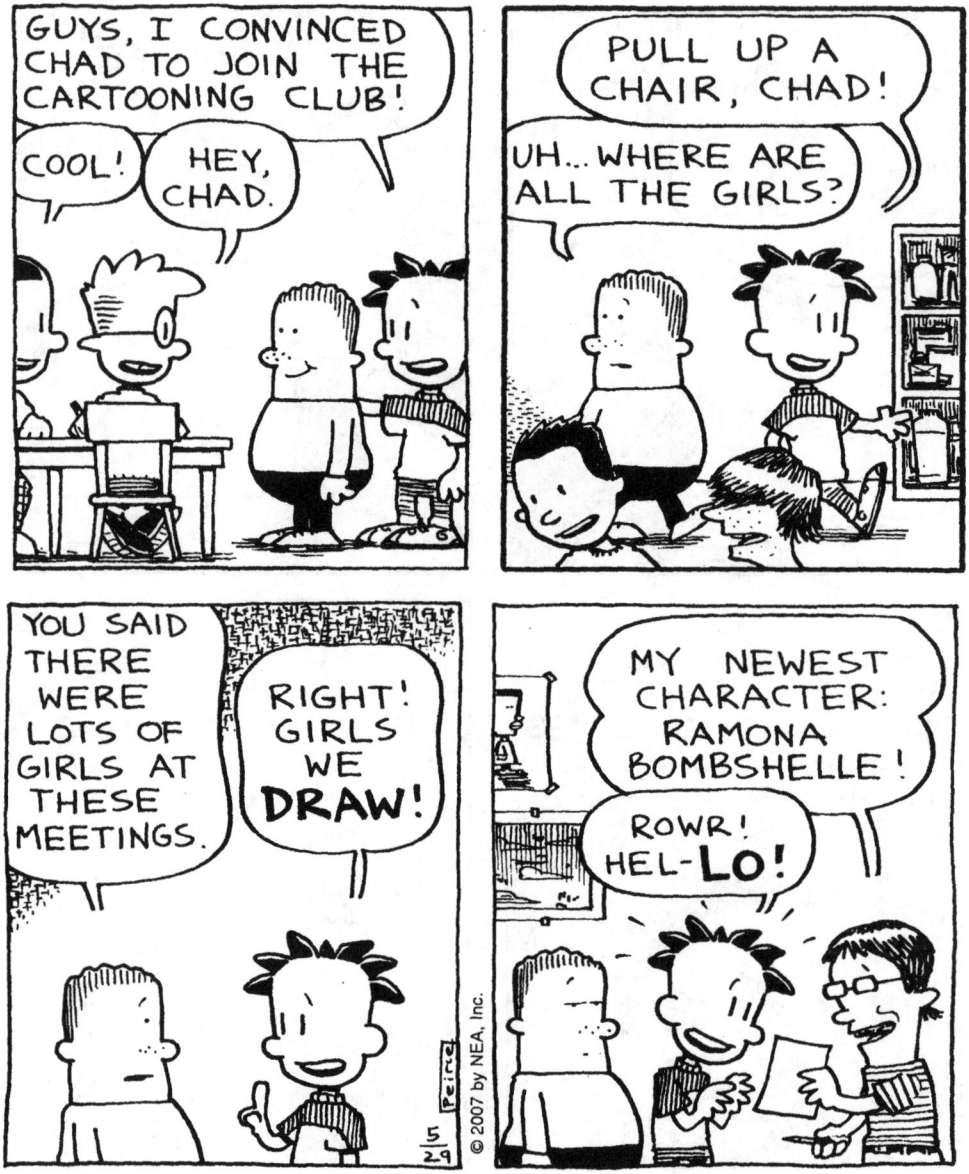

© 2007 by NEA, Inc.

© 2007 by NEA, Inc.

I NEED A SOUND EFFECT. WHAT DOES A GARBAGE DISPOSAL SOUND LIKE?
SORT OF LIKE: KRPBLKRPB!
YES! YES! THAT'S PERFECT!
HOW DO YOU SPELL THAT?
JUST LIKE IT SOUNDS.
© 2007 by NEA, Inc.

© 2007 by NEA, Inc.

© 2007 by NEA, Inc.

TIME, PEOPLE! HAND 'EM IN!
WRITE WRITE WRITE WRITE WRITE WRITE

THANK YOU, NATE.
GRUMBLE...

HOW'D YOU DO?
I THOUGHT IT WAS EASY! REALLY EASY!
ME TOO!

WHAT'D YOU THINK, NATE?
HM?

OH!... UH... YEAH!... IT WAS EASY! SO EASY!

HEH! I SURE HOPE THE FINAL IS THAT EASY!

THAT WAS THE FINAL.

COMIN' THROUGH.

© 2007 by NEA, Inc.

© 2007 by NEA, Inc.

© 2007 by NEA, Inc.

© 2007 by NEA, Inc.

© 2007 by NEA, Inc.

© 2007 by NEA, Inc.

SIR? I HAVE A NOTE FOR YOU FROM NATE WRIGHT.
FROM NATE WRIGHT?
ITALY
MR. NICHOLS

HE DROPPED IT OFF ON HIS WAY TO CLASS.
ALL RIGHT THEN. THANK YOU, MRS. SHIPULSKI.
RIP

Dear Principal Nichols,
Hi there, big guy. I hope your morning is going OK so far.

I just want to take a moment to let you know what a great principal you are. You do an awesome job as the leader of our school.

You inspire confidence and make us feel safe. And speaking of safety, I couldn't help noticing we haven't had a fire drill recently.

So, could we have a fire drill this morning? And could it happen at precisely 9:30?
MR. NICHOLS

Thanks! Sincerely,
Nate Wright
CLUNK!

YOU HAVE FORTY MINUTES TO COMPLETE THIS TEST. BEGIN.
I SHOULD HAVE INCLUDED A BRIBE.
Peirce

© 2007 by NEA, Inc.

© 2007 by NEA, Inc.

© 2007 by NEA, Inc.

© 2007 by NEA, Inc.

© 2007 by NEA, Inc.

© 2007 by NEA, Inc.

CHECK THIS OUT.
HEY NATE: WHO WAS THE MVP OF SUPER BOWL XV?
JIM PLUNKETT.
WHAT TEACHER DOES LINUS HAVE A CRUSH ON IN "PEANUTS"?
MISS OTHMAR.
WHAT'S JACKIE CHAN'S REAL NAME?
CHAN KONG-SANG.
WHAT YEAR WAS ZZ TOP INDUCTED INTO THE ROCK AND ROLL HALL OF FAME?
2004.
WHO DIRECTED "NACHO LIBRE"?
JARED HESS.
WHAT'S TWELVE TIMES SEVEN?
UHHH...
WAIT. LET ME THINK.
FASCINATING.
IT ALSO WORKS WITH STATE CAPITALS.

© 2007 by NEA, Inc.

© 2007 by NEA, Inc.

© 2007 by NEA, Inc.

© 2007 by NEA, Inc.

© 2007 by NEA, Inc.

© 2007 by NEA, Inc.

AHH, SUMMER!

NO SCHOOL TO THINK ABOUT! NO TEACHERS TO BOSS US AROUND! WE'RE FREE!

WE CAN DO ANYTHING WE WANT! THE POSSIBILITIES ARE ENDLESS! IT'S A BIG WORLD OUT THERE!

! MR. GALVIN!
YOU'RE JAYWALKING, BOYS. USE THE CROSS-WALK.

FIND SOMEWHERE ELSE TO PLAY FRISBEE, BOYS. YOU MIGHT HIT SOMEONE.
PRINCIPAL NICHOLS!

HOW'S THAT OFF-SEASON CONDITIONING PROGRAM GOING, LADIES?
COACH JOHN!

IF YOU WANT TO HAVE A PRAYER OF COMPLETING THE SUMMER READING LIST, I SUGGEST YOU HEAD FOR THE LIBRARY.

IT MIGHT BE A BIG WORLD, BUT IT'S A SMALL, SMALL TOWN.
I CAN'T WAIT TO GO OFF TO COLLEGE.
Peirce

© 2007 by NEA, Inc.

© 2007 by NEA, Inc.

© 2007 by NEA, Inc.

© 2007 by NEA, Inc.

© 2007 by NEA, Inc.

© 2007 by NEA, Inc.

WHAT'S WITH THE STICK?
JUST MAKING A POINT, TEDDY.
I KEEP TELLING COACH THAT NOTHING EVER HAPPENS OUT HERE IN RIGHT FIELD!
TO PROVE MY POINT, I'M MARKING THIS SPOT!
...AND I'LL BET I WON'T HAVE TO MOVE FROM THIS SPOT FOR THE WHOLE GAME!
CRACK!
WELL! LOOKS LIKE I WILL HAVE TO MOVE!
OOP! IT'S NOT CARRYING LIKE I THOUGHT IT WOULD!
ARRGH! NOW THE WIND'S TAKING IT!
THE SUN'S IN MY EYES! WHERE IS IT?
THERE IT IS!
NAB!
Peirce

© 2007 by NEA, Inc.

© 2007 by NEA, Inc.

© 2007 by NEA, Inc.

© 2007 by NEA, Inc.

© 2007 by NEA, Inc.

© 2007 by NEA, Inc.

"POOR NATE'S ALMANAC"? WHAT'S THIS?
I'M FOLLOWING IN THE FOOT-STEPS OF BEN FRANKLIN, BOYS!
POOR NATE'S ALMANAC $2

BACK IN THE 1700S, OL' BEN PUBLISHED "POOR RICHARD'S ALMANACK"!

IT WAS FILLED WITH ALL SORTS OF WISE SAY-INGS LIKE "THE EARLY BIRD GETS THE WORM" AND "A PENNY SAVED IS A PENNY EARNED"!

"POOR NATE'S ALMANAC" IS THE SAME THING, ONLY **BETTER!** YOU WON'T BELIEVE ALL THE WIS-DOM IN HERE!

AND THESE ARE MY LAST TWO COPIES! A BARGAIN AT TWO BUCKS EACH!
OKAY, I'LL TAKE ONE.
ME TOO!

HEY! THIS THING'S **BLANK!**
WAIT, THERE'S SOMETHING WRITTEN ON THE LAST PAGE.
FLIP FLIP FLIP

There's a sucker born every minute.

© 2007 by NEA, Inc.

© 2007 by NEA, Inc.

© 2007 by NEA, Inc.

© 2007 by NEA, Inc.

© 2007 by NEA, Inc.

© 2007 by NEA, Inc.

AARRGH!
4
WHAT HAPPENED? DID I JERK MY HEAD UP?
NOPE
DID I ROLL MY WRISTS?
NOPE
WAS I PAST HORIZONTAL ON MY BACKSWING?
NO
DID MY FRONT HIP FLY OPEN?
NO
DID I TURN MY SHOULDERS TOO EARLY?
NOPE
I DON'T GET IT. WHAT DID I DO WRONG?
WHAT DID I DO WRONG?
YOU HIT YOUR BALL INTO THE WOODS.
WRONG ANSWER.
KEEP LOOKING.

© 2007 by NEA, Inc.

© 2007 by NEA, Inc.

© 2007 by NEA, Inc.

© 2007 by NEA, Inc.

© 2007 by NEA, Inc.

© 2007 by NEA, Inc.

THREE MORE, AND YOU'LL BREAK YOUR ALL-TIME RECORD!
NO PROB-LEM!
SWISH!
TWO MORE! THAT'S PRESSURE SHOOTING!
"PRESSURE"? WHAT IS THIS "PRESSURE" YOU SPEAK OF?
SWISH!
I DON'T EVEN KNOW THE MEANING OF PRESSURE!
HELLO, BOYS.
MRS. GODFREY!
ULP!
I'M ON MY WAY OVER TO A READING AT THAT NEW BOOKSTORE!
HM.
UH HUH
OH, BUT I DIDN'T MEAN TO IN-TERRUPT YOU! KEEP SHOOT-ING, NATE!
UH... OKAY.
CLANG!
TSK! SO CLOSE!
NOW DO YOU KNOW THE MEAN-ING OF PRESSURE?
OH, HOW I HATE HER.
Paine

© 2007 by NEA, Inc.

© 2007 by NEA, Inc.

© 2007 by NEA, Inc.

© 2007 by NEA, Inc.

© 2007 by NEA, Inc.

© 2007 by NEA, Inc.

FRANCIS! DO YOU BELIEVE IN OMENS?
I GUESS SO.
WELL, IF I MAKE THIS SHOT, IT'S AN OMEN THAT I'M GOING TO BE RICH!
IF I MAKE IT WITHOUT HITTING THE BACKBOARD, IT MEANS I'M GOING TO BE FAMOUS!
...AND IF I MAKE IT WITHOUT HITTING THE BACKBOARD OR THE RIM, IT MEANS I'M GOING TO MARRY A SUPER-MODEL!
FLING!
CLANG!
CRASH!
MYOWR!
Screeee...
THUMP!
WHAT IF YOU MISS, AND THEN THE BALL BREAKS A WINDOW, HITS A CAT, ROLLS INTO THE STREET, AND GETS RUN OVER BY A DUMP TRUCK?
THEN IT'S A PRACTICE SHOT.

© 2007 by NEA, Inc.

© 2007 by NEA, Inc.

© 2007 by NEA, Inc.

© 2007 by NEA, Inc.

© 2007 by NEA, Inc.

© 2007 by NEA, Inc.

HERE YA GO, KID.
THANKS!
SLUP!

NO, SPITSY! BACK OFF! THIS IS MINE!
WURF!

I SAID NO, YOU FLEABAG! I'M NOT SHARING MY ICE CREAM!

AND DON'T ASK ME TO BUY YOU ONE OF YOUR OWN, EITHER! I'M OUT OF MONEY!
WOORF?

WHIMPER...
SIGH...

ALL RIGHT, ALL RIGHT... GIVE ME THAT TENNIS BALL.

FRANCIS.
HM?

CATCH.
GAH!

DON'T SAY I NEVER DO ANYTHING NICE FOR YOU.
SLORPF
SLORPF
SLORPF
SLORPF
SLORPF

© 2007 by NEA, Inc.

DAD, LET ME GIVE IT TO YOU STRAIGHT: I'M NOT SURE YOU'RE READY TO RUN A 10K.
OH, COME ON, NATE!
YOU ACT AS IF I'M TOTALLY INEXPERIENCED! I'LL HAVE YOU KNOW THAT I WAS A MEMBER OF MY HIGH SCHOOL TRACK TEAM!
YEAH, I KNEW THAT.
YOU DID?
I'VE SEEN YOUR YEARBOOK.
YOU HAVE?
8/7
HE WAS THE EQUIPMENT MANAGER.
BUSTED.
© 2007 by NEA, Inc.

© 2007 by NEA, Inc.

© 2007 by NEA, Inc.

© 2007 by NEA, Inc.

DAD, WHAT ARE YOU DOING?
CARBO LOADING!
MUNCH SLURP
ACCORDING TO ALL THE ARTICLES, NOTHING BEATS A BIG PLATE OF PASTA FOR A PRE-RACE MEAL!
YOU'RE SUPPOSED TO CARBO LOAD THE NIGHT BEFORE YOU RUN!!
OH.
IT'S 7:00 A.M., DAD. YOUR RACE STARTS IN AN HOUR.
EXACTLY. SO I'M TRYING TO EAT FAST.
NARF NARF
© 2007 by NEA, Inc.
8/11

ARRGH!
WHAT'S UP, DAD?

I'VE BEEN TRYING TO FIGURE OUT THIS BRAIN TEASER FOR AN HOUR!

MAY I ?
BE MY GUEST. IT'S IMPOSSIBLE!
MM.... MMM HMM...

GOT IT. THE SISTERS WERE BORN IN THIS ORDER: ELEANOR, EILEEN, ELIZABETH, EMILY AND EVELYN.

THAT WAS THE EASIEST BRAIN TEASER I'VE EVER SEEN.

THE PROBLEM WITH TEASING IS THAT IT OFTEN LEADS TO OUTRIGHT HUMILIATION.
Peirce

© 2007 by NEA, Inc.

© 2007 by NEA, Inc.

© 2007 by NEA, Inc.

© 2007 by NEA, Inc.

© 2007 by NEA, Inc.

© 2007 by NEA, Inc.

WANT TO KNOW, ONCE AND FOR ALL, WHY CATS ARE BETTER THAN DOGS?
NOT REALLY.

THEY'RE MORE AGILE! COMPARED TO CATS, DOGS ARE SLOW AND CLUMSY!

HERE'S AN EXAMPLE: IF YOU DROPPED A CAT UPSIDE DOWN FROM A SECOND-FLOOR WINDOW, WHAT WOULD HAPPEN?
IT WOULD LAND ON ITS FEET!

NOW!... WHAT WOULD HAPPEN IF YOU DROPPED A DOG UPSIDE DOWN FROM THAT VERY SAME SECOND-FLOOR WINDOW?

IT WOULD LAND ON THE CAT.

HIGH FIVE!
THAT'S WHY YOU DROP THE CAT FIRST!
Peirce

© 2007 by NEA, Inc.

© 2007 by NEA, Inc.

© 2007 by NEA, Inc.

© 2007 by NEA, Inc.

© 2007 by NEA, Inc.

© 2007 by NEA, Inc.

CALEB, MY YOUNG FRIEND! WANT TO BUY A CARICATURE?
WHAT ARE CARICATURES?
CARICATURES $1

YOU KNOW, CARTOONY PORTRAITS OF PEOPLE!
OOH! I'M PRETTY GOOD AT THAT MYSELF!

HERE'S ONE OF MY SISTER RENATA...
....LUKE SKYWALKER WITH OBI-WAN KENOBI...
...AND HERE! JACK SPARROW FROM "PIRATES OF THE CARIBBEAN"!
WELL... UH... KOFF!... THESE ARE OKAY, CALEB, BUT...

WOW, NATE! DID YOU DO THOSE?
THEY'RE GOOD!

HOW MUCH FOR THE PIRATE?
CARICATURES $1

UHHH...
CARICATURES $1
CARICATURES $2.00
Peirce

© 2007 by NEA, Inc.

© 2007 by NEA, Inc.

© 2007 by NEA, Inc.

© 2007 by NEA, Inc.

© 2007 by NEA, Inc.

© 2007 by NEA, Inc.

GAAH!

WHAT IS IT, NATE?
OH, MAN! WHAT A HORRIBLE NIGHTMARE!

MRS. GODFREY WAS IN IT!... AND SHE WAS LIVING HERE IN OUR HOUSE, AND...

EASY, SON. YOU'RE STRESSED ABOUT SCHOOL STARTING UP AGAIN, THAT'S ALL.

TELL YOU WHAT: JUST RELAX, AND I'LL BRING YOU A MUG OF HOT COCOA!
OKAY. THANKS, DAD.

WE'RE OUT OF COCOA...

GAAH!
HOW ABOUT A NICE TALL GLASS OF ASPARAGUS JUICE?

© 2007 by NEA, Inc.

© 2007 by NEA, Inc.

SO! AMANDA! YOU MUST BE NEW HERE!
YEAH, MY PARENTS ARE IN THE ARMY, SO WE MOVE AROUND A LOT.
9/5
WELL, IF YOU HAVE ANY QUESTIONS, JUST ASK ME, YOUR TRUSTY LOCKER PARTNER!
I WILL! THANKS, NATE!
I... I'M LOCKER PARTNERS WITH A HOTTIE!
Peirce
© 2007 by NEA, Inc.
I'M LOCKER PARTNERS WITH A HOTTIE!!
...AND WHAT A LUCKY, LUCKY GIRL SHE IS.
Cloud 9

© 2007 by NEA, Inc.

© 2007 by NEA, Inc.

I'M SORRY, NATE, BUT I CAN'T BE LOCKER PARTNERS WITH YOU ANYMORE.
WHAT?
9/8
AFTER ONE DAY?
WELL, I'M GOING OUT WITH JEREMY NOW, AND HE FEELS WEIRD ABOUT ME LOCKERING WITH ANOTHER BOY.
SO... HE'S THREATENED BY ME?
Reinel
GUYS! I'M A THREAT!
IN MANY, MANY WAYS.
© 2007 by NEA, Inc.

RED SOX.
YANKEES.
RED SOX!
YANKEES!

RED SOX!
YANKEES!

HEY! MISTER!

RED SOX OR YANKEES?

WASHINGTON SENATORS, BY CRACKY!

"BY CRACKY"?
THAT'S OLD SCHOOL RIGHT THERE.
Peirce

© 2007 by NEA, Inc.

I HATE SOCIAL STUDIES! MRS. GODFREY IS SO...
NATE, I'VE TOLD YOU THIS BEFORE...
I WILL NOT DISCUSS OTHER TEACHERS WITH STUDENTS! THAT'S ALL THERE IS TO IT!
YOU DON'T HAVE TO DISCUSS HER. YOU JUST HAVE TO LISTEN TO ME DISCUSS HER!
© 2007 by NEA, Inc.
OKAY. FIRST OF ALL, HER CLASSROOM SMELLS LIKE EGG SALAD...
9/11
Peirce

I WONDER IF MRS. GODFREY IS A JERK ALL THE TIME, OR ONLY DURING SCHOOL.
LET'S FIND OUT.

MR. ROSA, WHAT'S MRS. GODFREY LIKE OUTSIDE OF SCHOOL?
SHE'S VERY NICE.

WHEN'S THE LAST TIME YOU SAW HER OUTSIDE SCHOOL?
UHH...
9/12

© 2007 by NEA, Inc.
SHE'S A JERK ALL THE TIME.
Peirce

© 2007 by NEA, Inc.

© 2007 by NEA, Inc.

© 2007 by NEA, Inc.

HI, MR. EUSTIS! WANT YOUR LEAVES RAKED?
LEAVES? NATE, THE LEAVES HAVEN'T EVEN FALLEN YET!
BUT WHEN THEY DO FALL, WILL YOU PAY ME TO RAKE THEM?
WELL, SURE, BUT...
EXCELLENT!
WHAT'S THAT?
iPOD
HEAD-PHONES...
...AND CRANK IT UP!
ZWIK!
FOOM!
HEAVY METAL?
CLAY AIKEN!
Peirce

© 2007 by NEA, Inc.

© 2007 by NEA, Inc.

© 2007 by NEA, Inc.

© 2007 by NEA, Inc.

© 2007 by NEA, Inc.

© 2007 by NEA, Inc.

I'LL COVER!
AND I'LL RUSH!

WHAT'S THE RUSH COUNT? FIVE MISSISSIPPI?
WHATEVER. DOESN'T MATTER.

DOESN'T MATTER?
RUSH WHENEVER YOU WANT.

THREE MISSISSIPPI, THEN!
SURE.
TWO MISSISSIPPI!
OKAY.

HIKE!

ONE MISSISSIPPI...

...TWO MISSISSIPPI!

GAH!
FSSST!

FLING!

MY MOM WAS THROWING OUT SOME PERFUME!
OOH! WHO SMELLS DREAMY?
Peirce

© 2007 by NEA, Inc.

© 2007 by NEA, Inc.

© 2007 by NEA, Inc.

© 2007 by NEA, Inc.

© 2007 by NEA, Inc.

© 2007 by NEA, Inc.

DAD? THE GUYS AND I ARE STARTING A BAND...

...AND I WAS WONDERING IF I COULD BORROW YOUR GUITAR.
WELL, SURE! I'LL GO GET IT!

COOL! THANKS, DAD!
HANG ON! LET ME GET SOME OF THE DUST OFF!

THAT'S OKAY, YOU DON'T HAVE TO...
OH, I DON'T MIND! IT'S NO TROUBLE!

UH...GREAT. NOW CAN I...?
JUST A SEC. IT NEEDS TUNING!

I'LL DO THAT LATER! I'LL JUST...
NONSENSE! I CAN'T GIVE YOU A GUITAR THAT'S OUT OF TUNE!

BUT THE GUYS ARE WAITING FOR ME, AND...
E...A... D...G... HMM HMM...
PLINK PLONK

TWO HOURS LATER...
HOW MANY ROADS MUST A MAN WALK DOWNN...?
CRIPES.
Peirce

© 2007 by NEA, Inc.

© 2007 by NEA, Inc.

© 2007 by NEA, Inc.

© 2007 by NEA, Inc.

10/5

© 2007 by NEA, Inc.

© 2007 by NEA, Inc.

YOU'RE THE NICKNAME CZAR, RIGHT? I HAVE A NEW NICKNAME FOR MRS. GODFREY!
LET'S HEAR IT.

"CRUELLA"! 'CAUSE, YOU KNOW, SHE'S SO MEAN!
HM. NOPE. SORRY, GUY.

THAT'S TOO STRAIGHT-FORWARD! A GOOD NICKNAME WORKS ON **MANY** LEVELS!
TAKE ONE OF MY FAVORITE NAMES FOR MRS. GODFREY: "DARK SIDE OF THE MOON"!

THE "DARK SIDE", OBVIOUSLY, REFERS TO MRS. GODFREY'S SOUL. SHE HAS TURNED TO THE DARK SIDE AND EMBRACED EVIL AS A WAY OF LIFE.

THE MOON, LIKE MRS. GODFREY, IS HUGE, INHOSPITABLE AND DEVOID OF BEAUTY.

AND FINALLY, THE MOON'S DARK SIDE IS EXTREMELY COLD – EXACTLY LIKE MRS. GODFREY, WHO HAS NO WARMTH OR KINDNESS.

KEEP TRYING, KID.
THE GREAT ONES MAKE IT LOOK SO EASY.

© 2007 by NEA, Inc.

© 2007 by NEA, Inc.

© 2007 by NEA, Inc.

© 2007 by NEA, Inc.

© 2007 by NEA, Inc.

KID, I MIGHT BE ABLE TO MAKE THAT LIP A LITTLE LESS NOTICEABLE WITH SOME CREATIVE LIGHTING!
HOP UP ON THAT STOOL, AND I'LL SEE WHAT I CAN...
10/13
Peirce
OOPS!
BUMP!
© 2007 by NEA, Inc.

HOW COME YOU GET TO BE NICKNAME CZAR?
HM?
I'M CHALLENGING YOU, NATE! I CAN COME UP WITH BETTER NICK-NAMES THAN YOU CAN!
WE'LL HAVE A CONTEST!
EACH OF YOU HAS TO COME UP WITH A NICKNAME ON THE SPOT FOR THE FIRST TEACHER WHO WALKS BY!
TEDDY AND I WILL JUDGE!
AND REMEMBER: A GOOD NICKNAME WORKS ON MANY LEVELS!
GUYS! COACH JOHN!
UMM... LET'S SEE HERE...
"FAST BREAK."
"FAST BREAK" IS A BASKETBALL TERM, WHICH IS OBVIOUSLY APPROPRIATE FOR COACH JOHN.
...BUT THE WORD "FAST" IS IRONIC, BECAUSE COACH JOHN IS SO SLOW.
ALSO, "FAST BREAK" IS A PLAY ON WORDS. WHEN YOU BREAK A FAST, YOU EAT. CLEARLY, COACH JOHN HAS BROKEN A FEW FASTS IN HIS DAY.
I KNOW WHEN I'M BEATEN.
LONG LIVE THE CZAR!
Peirce

© 2007 by NEA, Inc.

© 2007 by NEA, Inc.

© 2007 by NEA, Inc.

© 2007 by NEA, Inc.

© 2007 by NEA, Inc.

© 2007 by NEA, Inc.

WHAT'S YOUR FAVORITE MOVIE?
I DUNNO.

YOU DON'T KNOW?
I HAVEN'T GIVEN IT MUCH THOUGHT.

WELL, WHAT ABOUT SONGS? WHAT'S YOUR FAVORITE SONG?
I LIKE LOTS OF SONGS.

BUT WHICH ONE DO YOU LIKE BEST?
I HAVE NO IDEA.

OKAY, THEN, COLORS! EVERYONE HAS A FAVORITE COLOR!
NOT ME.

OH, COME ON, FRANCIS! THERE'S GOT TO BE A COLOR YOU LIKE! JUST PICK ONE!

KLUNK!

SPLOOSH!

RED.

© 2007 by NEA, Inc.

© 2007 by NEA, Inc.

© 2007 by NEA, Inc.

GOOD NEWS, GUYS! MY DAD'S LETTING ME THINK UP A MIDDLE NAME FOR MYSELF!
I'M STILL MULLING IT OVER, BUT A CLEAR FRONT-RUNNER HAS EMERGED!
LET'S HEAR IT.
"MAXIMUS"!
10/25
VERY MODEST.
IS THAT A NAME OR A MALE ENHANCEMENT SUPPLEMENT?
© 2007 by NEA, Inc.

© 2007 by NEA, Inc.

© 2007 by NEA, Inc.

YOU KNOW WHAT, TEDDY? FRANCIS DOESN'T HAVE A FAVORITE MOVIE.
YOU DON'T?

THAT'S WEIRD, DUDE.
THAT'S WHAT I SAID!
WHY IS THAT SO WEIRD?

MOST PEOPLE HAVE A FAVORITE MOVIE, THAT'S ALL.
EVERYBODY DOES!
OKAY, OKAY! IF IT'S THAT IMPORTANT, I'LL PICK ONE!

MY FAVORITE MOVIE IS "CASABLANCA"! SATISFIED?

OH, YEAH! THE ONE WITH THOSE ZOO ANIMALS?
...AND THEY WIND UP IN AFRICA!
NO, NO, NO! THAT'S "MADAGASCAR"!

"CASABLANCA" IS A CLASSIC! THE AMERICAN FILM INSTITUTE RANKS IT THE SECOND GREATEST FILM OF ALL TIME!
HUH.
NEVER HEARD OF IT.

MY FAVORITE IS "DUMB AND DUMBER"!
HEY! SAME HERE!

REMEMBER HARRY'S BATHROOM SCENE?
HILARIOUS!
HERE'S LOOKING AT YOU, KID.
Peirce

© 2007 by NEA, Inc.

© 2007 by NEA, Inc.

© 2007 by NEA, Inc.

© 2007 by NEA, Inc.

© 2007 by NEA, Inc.

© 2007 by NEA, Inc.

ALL RIGHT, SPITSY, PAY ATTENTION! I'M GOING TO TEACH YOU HOW A REAL DOG ACTS!
WAG WAG WAG

SEE THIS? DOG! THAT'S YOU!
WURF!

...AND THIS? CAT! THE ENEMY!

NOW FOCUS, SPITSY! DOG CHASES CAT! GET IT?

...AND LOOK! THERE GOES A REAL LIVE CAT!!

WHAT DO YOU DO, SPITSY? WHAT DO YOU DO?
! !

NAB!
ZIP!

WURF! WOOF WOORF! WURF!
Peirce